Layman's to the English Constitution

by Albert Burgess

Dedicated to all those who suffered or forfeited their lives opposing tyrannical government whether by foreign occupying powers, dictatorships, kings, or even democratically elected governments ignoring constitutional constraints. It is only through determined resistance to tyranny that constitutions were ever developed in the first place.

Orinoco standard
Published by David Barnby, Witney
davebarnby@aol.com
Copyright © 2011

"Government has no right to make itself a party in any debate respecting the principles or modes of forming, or of changing, constitutions. It is not for the benefit of those who exercise the powers of government, that constitutions, and the governments issuing from them, are established. In all those matters, then rights of judging and acting are in those who pay, and not those who receive".

"A constitution is the property of a nation, and not those who exercise government"

Thomas Paine

CONTENTS

Introduction	Page 1
The origins of our Constitution	1
William I	4
William II	4
John	5
The Great Charta 1215	6
Important Constitutional Rulings	7
Henry III	7
Edward II	8
Edward III	8
Richard II	9
The Tudors	10
The Petition of Rights	11
The Grand Remonstrance	11
Declaration of Rights	12
The Bill of Rights 1689	13
Treason and Sedition	14
Finance Bill 1910, Parliament Act 1911	15
Hereditary Peerage	16
The Dispensing Power	19
Treason Act 1695	20
William Joyce	20
Henry VIII Powers	21
History of the Royal Assent	21
Nationality	23
Allegiance	24
Parliament, Stockdale vs. Hansard	25
Parliament is Supreme	25
Conclusion	27
Bibliography and further reading	

Introduction

Know your Constitution or lose your ancient freedoms

I believe that there is a need for a layman's guide to the English Constitution because the Government's guide to our Constitution: *'Inside Britain – A Guide to the UK Constitution'*, is a work designed to mislead the ordinary man, woman and child in this country. It allows them to enslave the subjects of her Majesty, undermine our culture and way of life and destroy a thousand years of history.

You should remember one thing; England is ruled, not by the Queen or by Parliament and not by the Queen *in* Parliament, England is ruled by the law of the very good Constitution left to us by our forefathers.

In every man and woman's life, there comes a time when their character is called into question; will they go with the flow no matter what, or will they say "No, this is not right" and "I will not have it?" The same is true of countries.

Our **Constitution** (simply meaning: *higher* law) is determined by the overriding will of the people. English people and their integrity can make a difference to matters seemingly beyond their control. This guide looks at moments in history which show how people have created the Constitution we have today. It also shows that all good monarchs recognise the importance of respecting the collective wishes of laymen to maintaining power. In other words, power truly is with the people, if only they would implement it.

The Origins of our Constitution

King Alfred the Great

Every work on the Constitution needs a starting point and I have chosen the year 841 because that was when King Alfred the Great was born. Alfred was the youngest son of King Ethelwulf by his first wife Osburh. He was sent to Rome at an early age to study. We can trace the formation of his character and love of learning to this early time in his life.

Alfred's life was not easy, and he spent most of his early years fighting the Danes. Each of his brothers became King in turn, and to each Alfred gave unswerving loyalty, until he inherited the Crown in 871. He became King of Wessex.

The Vikings were attacking and Alfred had to take control of his army at the same time as he was mourning the loss of his brother King Aethelred. Alfred was also affected by an illness. He could hardly have picked a worse time to become King; he was ill and a Viking army was at his door banging to get in.

In figure 1, we see Alfred hiding from the Vikings in the home of a peasant woman. He was asked to watch the cakes, but his troubled mind wandered and he forgot all about them. The cakes were all burnt and Alfred was scolded by the peasant woman when she returned. After this event his fortune began to change....

Figure 1: Alfred burns the cakes

Alfred managed to defeat the Viking army and established his Kingdom from Watling Street to the South Coast. He made his Kingdom capable of defending itself by building a strong navy to defeat the Viking long ships at sea. He built fortified towns and set up a form of national service so that half the men were in arms and the others worked the land. In doing so, he was able to defend the towns until a larger army could be mustered to come to their aid.

He became the only Saxon King to maintain full control of his Kingdom, so he became known as 'King of all the English'.

It was not only Alfred's ability as a war leader which earned him the title 'Great'. He set out to educate all his people, including the elderly. An Ealdorman who could not, or would not learn, was retired and replaced by a younger man.

It is in the field of law that we owe most to Alfred. He visited all the old kingdoms and took the best laws and customs from each of them. **Custom** is a practice that has been in use from times of greatest antiquity, with the approval of the people. By its very nature custom cannot be repealed, as it is the rule of the land and its people. Alfred recorded these laws and customs in a book he called *'The Dome'* (taken from *Doom* meaning punishment). Each of Alfred's Laws was based on the teachings of the Holy Bible.

Alfred showed *The Dome* to the **Witan** (councillors of a Saxon king) who agreed that it contained good law. It was issued throughout Alfred's England as the King's Law. It was not until his grandson **Athelstan** united the whole of England under one King that Alfred's Law covered the whole Kingdom of England. It is because of his book of law that Alfred is still held in the hearts and minds of English people.

Alfred had witnessed his father and brother's rule, so he had a strong sense of how to manage his Kingdom. He had decided upon a suitable candidate for Archbishop but the Pope had other ideas, sending him an Archbishop from Rome. Alfred returned the Pope's choice but the Pope sent him back to Alfred again with a messag: he, the Pope, appointed every king in the world, and if Alfred wanted to remain King he would have to accept the Archbishop chosen by him. Despite this, Alfred sent the Archbishop back to the Pope with another message: that he was elected King by the English and would do what was in their best interest. This incident began England's refusal to accept any foreign interference.

William I (Conqueror)

In October 1066, Duke William of Normandy followed up on a claim to the English Crown, which he asserted had been promised him by King Edward the Confessor who had died in the previous year, and invaded England. King Harold who had been crowned earlier that year was killed at the place which is

Figure 2: the coronation of William the Conqueror

still known as Battle, near Hastings, in Sussex. William chose to maintain the Laws of Edward the Confessor (which were Alfred's Laws), rather than introduce laws from his native Country of Normandy. The longevity of the Legal System created by Alfred the Great shows it to have been a success.

William II (Rufus)

William II believed he ruled by divine right and could do whatever he wished. As a result he ruled outside the confines of English law. William Rufus was shot through the heart with

Fig 3: Death of William Rufus

an arrow; which was considered to be an accident, although who knows?

In 1100, Henry I came to the throne. He also believed he could rule by divine right. He was very quickly disillusioned by the Barons and forced to issue the Charter of Liberties, a restatement of Alfred's Law.

Figure 4: Henry I

English Monarchs are subject to the law of the land

John

In 1213, King John (a very bad and unpopular King), was having a great deal of trouble from the Barons and the population generally. He had been using foreign mercenaries to suppress the population because his own soldiers refused to do so. And he so enraged the Barons by taking advantage of their wives, that fearing for his own safety, he handed over England to Archbishop Pandolph, the Papal Legate; receiving it back again to rule as a vassal king to

Figure 5: John kneeling before the Pope's Legate

the Pope for payment of 1000 marks a year.

Figure 6: Rage of John after signing the Magna Charta

John also took on the mantle of a crusader, so that anyone who attacked him would face excommunication.

The Great Charta 1215

John was forced to meet the Barons and thousands of the freemen of England at Runneymede in 1215. Here, he was then made to sign the **Great Charta** (also known as the **Magna Carta**), which was a restatement of the Charter of Liberties of Henry I (yet another restatement of Alfred's Laws). The Magna Carta was made by all the Estates of England; the King, the Barons, and the freemen of England and therefore it can

Figure 7: Henry III

only be undone by all the Estates of England meeting again.

Consequently, it is beyond the reach of Parliament.

King John died in 1216. His son, King Henry III, was a minor and John had appointed as his guardian the Earl of Pembroke, one of those who had supported King John in surrendering England to the Pope. On reaching the age where he was able to rule in his own right, King Henry III informed the Pope that, he, Henry, was the sole arbiter of all things to do with the church in England, and that he answered directly to God and not to the Pope. Henry ceased paying the 1000 marks a year to the Pope and rejected the Pope's claim that he was a vassal king to Rome. The Earl of Pembroke was, with the others who had assisted King John in surrendering England to the Pope, tried as a traitor and dealt with according to law. It must be said that the vast majority of the barons refused to accept the Pope's authority

Important early Constitutional legal rulings

Henry III

In the reign of Henry III, a man called Chief Justice **Henry de Bracton** was on the King's Bench. Bracton's rulings are so important that they are still taught at law schools today. He said:

"That the King is beneath no man, but he is beneath God, and rules England as God's Lieutenant and according to Gods laws. And he is beneath the law for it is by the law that he becomes King".

This judgment imposes constraints on the sovereign so that he cannot act unjustly.

Another of Bracton's rulings is:

"The laws of England, having been approved by those who use them, and having been confirmed by the Oaths of Kings, cannot be changed or disposed of without the common consent of those by whose council and consent they were promulgated."

For those who are unaware: our forefathers established the principle that it is the English people who must approve any changes to our laws, and this principle has been handed down to us.

In England we have the Rule of Law; unjust laws are not laws.

In 1345, Chief Justice Stonor said, *"Law is that which is right."*

In the second half of the same century, Judge Hilary said:

"We will not and we cannot change the Ancient usages."

Chief Justice Beresford said:

"You should not only look at the letter of the law, but at the spirit of the law."

Beresford also said:

"There is no such thing as a bad law, for if it is bad, it is not law."

It is to judges like these, that those good sound principles espoused by the Common Law of England owe so much.

Englishmen have had just cause to feel safe under English Law. King Edward III issued **The Statute of Treason, Provisors and Praemunire (1351).**

These were anti-papal laws, which were designed to keep foreign interference out of England. The ultimate legal defence of Crown and Realm depended on the Treason Law.

Edward II

Edward II was another King who thought he could do as he liked. He was lazy when it came to his duties as King, and he had his favourites who almost seemed to get away with everything. This caused the Barons to remove Edward, who was forced to resign his Crown in favour of his son. He was then killed in Berkeley Castle in Gloucestershire with a red hot poker up his back passage.

Edward III

In 1366, King Edward III received a letter from the Pope demanding 1000 marks a year for every year that it had not been paid, and threatening action if the monies were not received. Edward III spoke to the bishops and the Lords, who spoke to the Commons.

Figure 8: Edward II being deposed

First the bishops, then the Lords, and finally the Commons came to Edward and told him that England had not been King John's to give away. Under English law, John had only held England in trust for his successors and therefore the agreement between the Pope and King John was not valid.

By giving England to the Pope,

John had broken the law. The money was not owed and should not be paid. This major constitutional ruling ensures that England's sovereigns were not and can never be, vassal Kings to anyone. This is a most important constitutional ruling which applies as much today as it did then.

When John Major came back from Maastricht and said the Queen was now a citizen of Europe, he attempted to destroy a constitutional principle; that our kings can never be vassal kings to anyone. Arguably, John Major had committed the major crime of High Treason.

King Edward III also claimed the Kingdom of France. Parliament made him sign an undertaking that, as King of France, Edward could have no say in how England was governed.

Richard II

In 1392, King Richard II issued his **Statute of Praemunire,**

Figure 9: Edward III

breaches of which amounted to High Treason. It was repealed in the **Criminal Law Act 1967,** just in time to prevent Edward Heath's Government committing praemunire by placing Her Majesty's Courts under the dominion of the European Courts.

I asked the Law Commission why this most important **Statute of Praemunire** had been repealed. The reason given to me by the Law Commission was that the law had not been used for many years and so they inferred it was obsolete. Yet there is no such thing as a principle of

Figure 10: Richard II insisting on his supremacy

Figure 11: Henry VIII

obsolescence in English law. Who is to say that it had not been used, because, like all law, it is designed to prevent crime? By preventing treasonable crimes from being committed, King Richard's Statute had worked very well.

The Tudors

Under King Henry VIII we see the final parting of the ways between the Roman Church and England. The 1351 Treason Act remained the predominant Treason Act.

During the reign of Queen Elizabeth I, the Pope attempted to have Queen Elizabeth murdered. He said that whoever killed her would not suffer, but would receive both earthly and heavenly rewards. Queen Elizabeth was understandably far from amused by this and she reissued her father's **Act of Supremacy** in 1559. This Act contained an Oath, part of which states:

"No Foreign Prince, Person. State or Potentate. Hath or ought to have any Power, Jurisdiction, Superiority, Supremacy, or Authority Ecclesiastical or Spiritual in this Realm."

Figure 12: Bishops acknowledge Elizabeth I

The Tudors on the whole ruled according to the prerogatives given to them by law.

The Stuarts

The Stuarts, on the other hand, believed they ruled by 'Divine

Figure 13: King Charles I summoned to execution

Right' and were answerable only to God. As a result, two out of the four Stuarts lost their crown; Charles I lost his crown *and* his head, then James II was forced to flee the Country to safety.

※

The Petition of Rights 1628

In 1628, Charles I was presented with the **Petition of Rights,** a restatement of Alfred's Law.

※

The Grand Remonstrance 1641

Later, in 1641, the **Grand Remonstrance** was a request by Parliament for Charles to rule according to the law (yet another restatement of Alfred's Law) but Charles refused. He was then put on trial for treason against the people, found guilty and executed. James II was told by Parliament that by attempting to catholicise the country he was acting illegally. James retaliated, dissolved Parliament, and carried on as before until he fled to France.

Figure 13: King Charles I summoned to execution

Declaration of Rights

William III of Orange

Prince William of Orange was asked by the now out of work politicians, if he would like the Crown, as his wife Mary was next in line to the throne. William and Mary would rule as joint sovereigns, because Mary said she would not be over her husband, and William said he would not be a servant of his wife.

William landed at Torbay with an army much smaller than that commanded by King

Figure 14: James II receiving the French bribe

James II. When James saw his army deserting in droves, he sent his wife and son to France and followed them a short while later.

William was asked to take on the administration of the Country. However, William despised the English, and replaced a number of our senior military and civil servants with Dutchmen. The politicians (thinking they had just got rid of one bad King and it looked like they were about to get another), went and spoke to the Alderman and fifty of the Common Council of the City of London. William hearing of this issued instructions for writs to be sent to every borough in England. The boroughs were to send representatives to Westminster to tell the politicians and William how we, the English, wished to be ruled.

The representatives came to Westminster and met the Lords, the politicians, the Aldermen and Common Council of the City of London at a Convention. It was not a parliament because only a King or Queen may call a parliament. King James II was in France and had no desire to call a parliament. After much discussion they produced the **Declaration of Rights**, which was further restatement of Alfred's laws. The Declaration was shown to William and Mary, who were told by the representatives of the people that, if they wanted the Crown, they had to accept the terms of the Declaration of Rights (these were the minimum rights and freedoms the people would tolerate). William and Mary accepted the Crown under these terms.

Now he was King, William called a Parliament. William did not have an election but,

Figure 15: The Crown being offered to William and Mary

instead, said the people's representatives would be his Parliament. The first thing Parliament did was to pass the **Declaration of Rights** into law as the **Bill of Rights 1689**. Two codicils were added to the Bill, first any amendments after the 23rd September 1689 were void and not lawful, and second, that this Bill was for all time.

✳

The Bill of Rights 1689

Now it is a convention that no parliament can bind another. So how could this Parliament bind every successive Parliament for ever? The answer is simple. This Parliament was made up of the people's representatives. The will of the people is supreme over both Parliament and the

Sovereign. Until such time as the representatives of the people meet and change the 1689 Bill of Rights, this Bill remains the law.

In his Commentaries on the Laws of England, **Chief Justice Blackstone** in 1765 said that he was writing about the laws of Alfred. This makes it clear that Alfred's Laws were still in place during the life of Chief Justice Blackstone.

Since the time of King Alfred, our law has developed for over a thousand years. It was developed by our forefathers because, from time to time, bad (or frankly useless) kings have needed to have their ways corrected. Kings who would not listen were removed. As mentioned above:

- Edward II was such a King and was removed in favour of his son. He was subsequently killed at Berkeley castle Gloucestershire.

- Charles I had his head removed for treason against the people, as did his Lord Strafford.

- James II was forced to flee to France.

Each and every time a king has been removed or had his ways changed, the reason has been because he has tried to rule outside the law - Alfred's Laws of England.

Treason and Sedition

We have dealt with English Constitutional law as it is written. The law does indeed give us protection from despotic government. Our forefathers, however, did not just trust the law. They built into our system of government extra safeguards, specifically in the way Parliament itself is required to work.

Parliament consists of three parts; the Commons, the Lords, Spiritual and Temporal, and the Sovereign, over all three parts. Individually none of these parts can make or repeal law. Our forefathers foresaw that if any one part was able to claim supremacy in the system, we would suffer from oppressive government. Parliament works by the Commons originating legislation, which is then passed to the Lords for scrutiny. It is the function of the Lords to refuse the legislation if they believe it to be oppressive, or in any other way not good legislation. If the Lords approve the legislation, it then goes before the Sovereign who may refuse the Royal Assent if he or she considers the legislation not to be in the best interests of their Subjects. Any attempt to subvert the make-up of Parliament is the major crime of sedition, and at this level, sedition is High Treason. Any attempt to damage the Sovereign's powers or authority is High Treason.

※

Finance Bill 1910 & the Parliament Act 1911

Such a situation occurred in 1910. The Asquith Government attempted to put through a **Finance Bill**. The Lords rejected the Bill because it imposed too high a tax burden on the Subjects.

Asquith went to the Lords and told them he was putting forward a Bill which would limit their authority to reject bills. If they did not pass this Bill, he proposed to put 500 new peers into the Lords, and they would vote for the closure of the Lords. The Lords gave their consent to the **Parliament Act 1911**, but under duress.

The Bill was presented to King Edward VII who refused Royal Assent, on the grounds that it removed a protection given to English Subjects by the Constitution. King Edward told Asquith he would have to ask the Country.

But shortly thereafter King Edward VII died and King George V came to the throne. He was told by a Government minister that, as King, he retained all his prerogatives. However, he could not use any of the Royal Prerogatives without the backing of a Government minister.

This ministerial advice has no basis in our

Constitution and amounts to a clear act of Treason. Furthermore, since it imagines the death of the King as a Sovereign King it is an act of High Treason under the terms of the Treason Act 1351.

※

Hereditary Peerage

Meanwhile, Asquith travelled around the Country telling everyone about the Lords refusal of consent to the Bill. He told the public this Bill would give them a pension, but failed to mention the tax burden it would impose upon them.

In one fell swoop, Asquith had neutered the power of the Lords to protect the Subject from bad law, and removed the right of sovereigns to refuse the Royal Assent to parliamentary bills.

Asquith was a Fabian. Arguably, the undeclared policy of the Fabians was the destruction of the Constitution and our way of life. Consequently, Asquith's actions amounted to a clear act of sedition, which, at this level, amounts to High Treason.

Subsequent Acts have continued to restrict the authority of the House of Lords. Finally, the plan to remove all but ninety two hereditary Peers was passed by Parliament in 1998. Currently, the Government plans to remove *all* hereditary Peers from the House of Lords.

Constitutionally a peer can only be removed by a bill after committing a serious crime. A separate bill is required for each peer before he can be removed. It is unconstitutional (and therefore illegal) to remove every hereditary peer in a General Bill. Baroness Ashton said in the House of Lords that a General Bill cannot be used to remove the hereditary peers.

Why do we want the hereditary peerage? Well, on

the whole, they were honest and honourable. They had large estates and money so they were most unlikely to take a bribe; they were also very protective of the family reputation. The Hereditary Peers are the traditional advisors to the Sovereign.

Her Majesty Queen Elizabeth II was taught Constitutional Law by a Fabian, **Henry Marten, and the Fabians, I believe, want to destroy our way of life.** Her Majesty will always do what her ministers say she must. **We are now governed by an elected dictatorship**. What has this treacherous dictatorship illegally achieved?

(1) Magna Charta and the **Bill of Rights** state that we cannot suffer any fine or forfeiture unless we have been found guilty of an offence in a court of law. Fines should not be excessive and no cruel or unusual punishments inflicted. **We now have a whole range of fixed penalty fines, for which we are not permitted to appeal in one of Her Majesty's Courts of Law.**

(2) The **Bill of Rights** says that any threat of a fine or forfeiture voids the offence. **Yet we are told that if we drop litter or don't have a TV licence we will be fined £1000. We are told that if we do not insure or tax our car it will be seized and crushed.**

(3) The **Bill of Rights** also states that we may not be imprisoned unless we have been found guilty of an offence in one of Her Majesty's Courts of Law. **Yet we now have 28 days detention under the anti- terrorism laws. In other words, detention without any evidence being produced to anyone, let alone one of Her Majesty's Courts of Law.**

These Constitutionally illegal laws are subverting the Constitution by the major crime of sedition, which, at this level, amounts to high treason against Her Majesty's Subjects.

(4) Edward Heath set up a

conspiracy to subvert our ancient Constitution, the major crime of Sedition. Sedition at this level is High Treason. Heath also conspired with others to hand over this Country to a foreign power, the EEC/EU - the major crime of High Treason. Every succeeding government has signed treaties with the EU surrendering our rights to govern ourselves under laws passed by the Queen in Parliament. In doing so, every government since the Heath government has committed the major crime of High Treason.

(5) The restrictions of the ability of the hereditary peerage to play their proper part in government, as defined by the Constitution, constitute the major crime of Sedition which at this level is High Treason.

(6) The removal of the hereditary peerage from the Lords constitutes an act of Sedition amounting to High Treason.

(7) A Minister from the Asquith Government advised King George V: that he keeps all his Royal Prerogatives, but may not use them unless he has the backing of a minister. This is to usurp the Royal Prerogative, which is an act of high treason.

It is a fundamental part of our Constitution that Parliament may not surrender any of their rights to govern to a foreign power, unless we have been defeated in war.

It is a fundamental part of our Constitution that a statute law cannot repeal by implied repeal a Constitutional law.

It is a fundamental part of our Constitution that, when a law is repugnant, or impossible to perform, the common law will intercede and strike it down. Parliament is governing outside the rule of the Constitutional law of England and Wales. Scotland has its own Constitution. I leave it to the people of Scotland to deal with government over breaches of the Scottish Constitution.

I do not want you to take my word for any of this. My teacher at school used to tell us to look it up, because then you will remember it, and I am saying to you look it up! In particular research: the **Legal Codes of Alfred**, the **Charter of Liberties** of Henry I (1100), the **Magna Charta (1215)**, the **Petition of Rights (1628)**, the **Grand Remonstrance (1641)**, and the **Bill of Rights (1689)**.

Then I want you to look out of the window and see just how thoroughly the Government is destroying the Constitutional Laws of England.

Now you understand how our ancient Constitution works… you have to choose whether you are going to roll over and become slaves or live as free born Englishmen like our forefathers; many of whom died to give us the rights and freedoms the world believes we enjoy.

I am not yet asking you to risk death. We are not anywhere near there yet. I am asking you to fight back. England is ruled by law. Parliament is ignoring the best laws in the history of the world. Let us use the law to get back that which is ours,

our Constitution and our Country. **Sedition** is any act designed to subvert the Constitution.

High Treason is any act designed to betray the Sovereign, Constitution and People of England.

Can you recognise these acts of betrayal by Parliament today?

※

On the dispensing power of the king to dispense with a penalty for an offence:

In 1674, Chief Justice Vaughn of the Common Pleas, ruled that the king cannot dispense with a penalty for a common law offence. The king can dispense with a penalty for a statute offence, but he cannot dispense with a penalty for all statute offences. The king cannot for example allow someone to commit murder. The king can dispense with a penalty when he is the victim, but he cannot dispense with a penalty when it affects a third party who could claim for damages in a court of law. The king cannot, for example, allow someone who has a duty to repair a bridge, avoid liability to anyone using the bridge. Because that would remove the right of anyone injured by walking over the bridge, due to its lack of repair, from claiming for damages against those whose duty it was to keep the bridge in good repair.

Queen Elizabeth I forgave the Earl of Essex for his personal treason against her, when he went to strike her with his sword. But she removed his head when his treason was against the state and her Subjects.

※

The Treason Act 1695

This act puts a three year time limit on bringing trials for treason. Bearing in mind the preceding explanation of the powers of dispensation available to the King, and the actions of Queen Elizabeth I, we can clearly see that this time limit is nonsensical in allowing someone who has committed treason to get away with it just because they are able to avoid arrest for three years. It is also ultra vires because the king cannot give the assent for what is a partial dispensation for an act of treason. When we all suffer a loss, should treason succeed?

We all of us have a right and a clear duty to prosecute those who commit this most serious crime. As such it is clearly constitutionally impossible for such a dispensation to be given.

※

William Joyce

William Joyce was an American citizen of Irish descent, who obtained a United Kingdom Passport, before running off to Nazi Germany on the outbreak of the Second World War. Joyce and his wife both made broadcasts in aid of the German war machine between 1939 and 1940 when his passport expired. Joyce was arrested by British Forces personnel in 1945, and he was put on trial and executed for treason in 1946, some six years after his last act of treason under the 1945 Treason Act. It was specifically brought in to try him and other known traitors.

※

Henry VIII Powers

King Henry VIII was an arrogant bully who ruled by dictate. The Bishop of Rochester upset his cook, one Richard Rose, who poisoned the meal and seventeen people died. King Henry VIII ordered the cook to be taken to Smithfield and boiled to death. Richard was duly boiled to death. This became known as a Henry VIII power. Parliament today claim to rule by Henry VIII powers. They evidence this by the 'blue eyed baby rule'. Parliament say that they could pass a law saying all blue eyed baby boys born in July were to be killed, that would be the law and the babies would be killed. Chief Justice Sir Edward Coke in 1628 said that "Parliament may sometimes pass a law which is against common right and reason, or repugnant or impossible to perform, and the Common Law would intercede and strike it down". I would hope we would all feel that any law which said we should kill anyone, let alone babies, was repugnant; because the families of these babies would fight, as would everybody else, to prevent the deaths of these children. It would be impossible to perform because the common man would enforce the Common Law of England by armed resistance if necessary.

※

The History of the Royal Assent

In the beginning there was no parliament but English Kings were not dictators, they all used advisors. These advisors made sure that the King did not rule outside the law. The Anglo Saxon kings had the Witan, made up of the Ealdormen and Thanes. Later the Norman French kings had a parliament made up of barons and the knights from the shires. For a long time Parliament met where the king was in the country, before it became settled at the Palace of Westminster. All our early kings and queens were in Parliament when it met, and were able to exert considerable influence on the actions of Parliament. The Stuarts believed they ruled by divine right. We know what happened to them.

King William III attended Cabinet meetings and the House of Lords. Queen Anne, like William, attended Cabinet meetings and the House of Lords; as a result, they both had a very clear idea of what was happening, both with government, and in the Country. Following the death of Queen Anne we had King George I. He spoke only German, and because he had no idea what was being said, he attended neither Cabinet meetings nor the House of Lords. This allowed the politicians to govern in his name, with the King having no say about what was done in his name.

Figure 16: Queen Anne

His son, King George II, spoke English, but was discouraged by the politicians from attending Cabinet meetings and the Lords. Indeed he complained that his ministers were kings in his Kingdom. He

Figure 17: George I

was effectively prevented from carrying out his role as King. George III was badly educated, his main interest being farming about which he was knowledgeable. He also suffered from mental ill health and, for a large part of his reign, was not competent to govern.

Figure 18: George II

This gave the politicians, purely by accident the idea that they could assume power without the sovereign having any say, or at most, not much, in what government did. It is this political power, taken without permission, not authority granted under the law that encourages

Figure 19: George III

governments to believe that those in the House of Commons can do anything they like, whether the Sovereign or the people like it or not. This is the situation we have today (see more below).

※

Nationality

The best description of nationality was given by King Edward III in his statute *25 E.3 de natis ultra mare.*

Edward ruled that everyone born under an English King is English, if you were born overseas of an English father you are English, if you are born of an English mother and an alien father you are alien. If an Englishman goes into the Country of an enemy, or into a friendly Country, and refuses to return to England on command of the King, the children born there are alien.

Allegiance

Who owes allegiance to the King? First, everyone who is born under the King, or who is born outside England to an English father. Second, those who accept English nationality. Third, anyone who comes to England to trade or otherwise, comes under the protection of the King whilst they are here. So, for instance, a French merchant trading in England would owe allegiance to the King as long as he is in England. A French soldier here as an invader, would owe no duty of allegiance to the King. A foreign prince who came to visit England, would owe no allegiance to the King, but would require the King's permission to land in England. Everyone over the age of 12 was required to swear an oath of allegiance to the King. It is believed this oath-taking was started by King Arthur, and goes back into the mists of time. The later Acts of Supremacy, add to this, but do not replace the Oath of Allegiance. It is English common law that the king cannot resign his Crown, nor can those estates in Parliament withdraw their homage. If the king was no king because he resigned, then those in Parliament were no Parliament if they withdraw their homage. If the throne were usurped, the rightful heir would still become king, though the usurper would be king in fact. Parliament has no right to take the Crown from the next in line and appoint another as king; to do that would be to usurp the Crown. The 1689 Declaration of Rights, made up of the representatives of the people, was able to remove the Stuart line because the will of the People is supreme over Parliament and the King.

Parliament, Stockdale vs. Hansard

In Stockdale vs. Hansard 1837, Stockdale, a book publisher, was libelled in the House of Commons, and that libel was published in Hansard. Chief Justice Denman found in favour of Stockdale and awarded him £600 damages. Judge Patterson, giving the opinion of the other eight judges in the case, ruled that:

'In the beginning, Parliament met under one roof with the Lords one side and the Commons the other, with the King at the head. At that time, Parliament was the highest court in the land and could not be sued in any other court. But, for their own reasons, the Houses chose to sit under different roofs. The House of Lords is where the law lords and the King sit, and it is the highest court in the land. But the House of Commons is in no way a court of law, and the common man must be able to sue the House of Commons in any of the courts in the land, for wrongs done to him by the actions of the House of Commons.'

Now that the Law Lords have been removed from the House of Lords, The House of Lords is no longer the highest court in the land; that role now falls to the Supreme Court.

Following the spirit of Judge Patterson's ruling, it means, in my opinion that the common man may now sue Parliament for wrongs done to him by the actions of Parliament as a whole.

※

Parliament is Supreme
(Parliament is Sovereign)

Or is it? If true, this would amount to surrendering to the Crown (in Parliament), all the rights and liberties of the people.

It is, of course, natural for political animals to hanker after power, and it's often stated: **'power corrupts and absolute power corrupts absolutely'**.

It was, as we have seen above, the **Declaration and Bill of Rights** that left the authority of kings as it had always been under the law, contracted to us by the Coronation Oath. However, politicians have opportunistically awarded themselves unlimited powers in its place, to the extent that they claim that Parliament can do as it pleases - **'blue eyed baby boy concept'** (see above).

The political classes have misused their skills and cunning to side-line the Constitution that limited their powers, so we now have an untenable situation where the public are faced with politicians who seem to subscribe to a new doctrine of the 'Divine Rights of Politicians'.

A breach of the limitation of the Crown in Parliament would be contrary to the law of Parliament. The 1st Earl of Chatham, Pitt the Elder, was aware of the threat when he said:

"..... instead of the arbitrary power of a Stuart king, we must submit to the arbitrary power of the House of Commons. If this be true, what benefit do we derive from the exchange? Tyranny my Lords, is detestable in every shape, but none so formidable as where it is assumed and exercised by a number of tyrants. My Lords, this is not the fact, this is not the Constitution, we have a law of Parliament. We have a Statute Book and the Bill of Rights".

No doubt it was the French Revolution that encouraged this power grab, but also this idea was predated by William Prynne who postulated the sovereignty of Parliament.

It was then enthusiastically taken up by Professor Dicey in 1885 without lawful authority. It is this concept, more than any that has led to the widespread view that we now live in an elected dictatorship.

With the strangling of the House of Lords, the removal of Royal Assent by the Monarch, and oftimes savage control of elected representatives, the executive is now virtually free to do as it wishes.

Parliament is not sovereign. It must abide by the rule of law, which includes the Bill of Rights. Betty Boothroyd, in the House of Commons in 1993, in reply to a matter of breach of privilege raised by Tony Benn stated:

"I am sure that the House is entitled to expect when the case referred to by the right hon. Gentleman begins to be heard on Monday, that the Bill of Rights will be required to be fully respected by all those appearing before the courts."

❊

Conclusions

In England we have a very good and ancient Constitution, built by the trials and tribulations of our forefathers, who experienced, on a number of occasions, despotic rule, which their desire to live as freemen gave them the strength to overcome. On each occasion they set in place protections to prevent despotic rule. Today we have despotic rule by the House of Commons, who claim authority even over Her Majesty the Queen. They have withdrawn their homage to Her Majesty and, under the Common Law of England, are no Parliament, but foul and base traitors. We must, like our Forefathers, find the strength to overcome this evil, and, make no mistake, it is Evil. They are destroying a legal system and Constitution built around the teachings of the Holy Bible.

In the House of Commons, according to the secretary of Andrew Dismore (MP), Dr Egan: "there has been an interesting discussion on whether by passing a law, they (Parliament), can do away with the rule of law". Why would anyone in their right mind even contemplate such a thing, let alone discuss it? What are we left with if they remove the rule of law? We are left with satanic law: "Do what thou wilt, shall be the whole of the law". So if your 12 year old child is raped it is not a crime! When your old mother is burgled and beaten to a pulp, it is not a crime. When a bank is robbed and a cashier shot to death it is not a crime. Make no mistake this is what our politicians have in mind for us. If only so that they can continue to 'rob us blind' with their expenses. Our forefathers protected our freedoms, and in doing so developed the most perfect constitution known to man.

Bibliography and further reading

Adams, G.B., and Stevens, H.M. eds., (1921), *'Select Documents of English Constitutional History'*. London: Macmillan and Co. Ltd.

Ashworth, P.A. ed., (1896), *'English constitutional history: From the Teutonic conquest to the present time'*. London: Stevens and Haynes.

Bede, (731), *'A History of the Church and the English people'*. Translated by L. Sherley-Price, and revised by R.E. Latham, 1974. Middlesex: Penguin Books Ltd.

Blackies, *'Blackie's comprehensive history of England'*. (Vol.5) London: Blackie and Son Ltd. Figure 12.

Cassell, *'Illustrated History of England'* (Vol.1), London: Cassell, Petter and Galpin. Figures 1-11.

Elton, G.R. ed., (1972), *'The Tudor Constitution: documents and commentary'*. Cambridge: University Press.

Feiling, K., (1959), *'A History of England: From the coming of the English to 1918'*.London: Macmillan and Co.

Green, J.R, (1902), *'A short history of the English people'*. (Vol.1-4), London: Macmillan and Co. Ltd.

Department of Constitutional Affairs, *'Inside Britain – A Guide to the UK Constitution'*.

Keynes, S., Lapidge, M., (2004), *'Alfred the Great: Asser's Life of King Alfred and other contemporary sources'*. London: Penguin books.

Macaulay, Lord., (1895), *'The History of England: From the accession of James II'*. (Vol.1), London: Longman's, Green and Co.

Maitland, F.W., (1908), *'The Constitutional History of England'*. Cambridge: University Press.

Robertson, C.G. Sir., (1947), *'Select Statutes, Cases and Documents to illustrate English constitutional history, 1660-1832'*. 8th Ed. London: Methuen and Co. Ltd.

Trevelyan, G.M., (1934), *'History of England'*. London: Longman's, Green and Co.

Stubbs, W., (1873), *'The Constitutional History of England: in its origin and development'*. 5th Ed. (Vol.1-3), Oxford: Clarendon Press.

Sturdy, D., (1995), *'Alfred the Great'*. London: Constable.

Hale, M. Sir the Prerogatives of the King. Seldom Society 1976

John Bingley, *'Unlawful Governance'*.

David Barnby, *'Shoe-horned into the EU'* - CD

Statutes

Act of Supremacy 1559

Criminal Law Act 1967

The Statute of Treason, Provisors and Praemunire 1351

The Statute of Praemunire 1392

The Treason Act 1351

The Parliament Act 1911